Plunge

Alice Jones

Apogee Press

Berkeley · California

2012

Acknowledgements

Earlier versions of the poems appeared in the following journals.

Narrative Magazine, "Departure"
Southwest Review, "Muddy Hollow"
Volt, "Real Time," part 1
ZYZZYVA, "The Forest"

The sestina from "Valle d'Aosta" won the 2006 Lyric Poetry Award from the Poetry Society of America.

Many thanks to Rusty Morrision and Patricia Dienstfrey for their comments.

Cover photography: *River, Bhutan* by YooChong Wong

Book cover and interior design by Philip Krayna at NKD
www.nkdesigngroup.com

ISBN 978-0-9787667-9-5. Library of Congress Catalog Card Number 2011941810.

Published by Apogee Press, 2308 Sixth Street, Berkeley CA, 94710.
www.apogeepress.com

Contents

Departure

1.

One grain on the tongue
silvering the horizon—
the body's green kiss.

2.

A blue rabbit pounds the moon
an old woman falls open

in the nightmare's silver,
you remember no horizon
or silty river delta

goodbye to this taste
the body's crossing.

3.

At the golden gates
a rabbit sinks in silver rice

a woman's bed
night's faded tint

the mouth complains
no grain of kindness

on the world's horizon.
Flannelled words

green river stooping
now a growl

coming to this mouth
a taste for falling

simple as kissing goodbye.

4.

In golden China
a bruised profile
at the horizon's gate

bedding down, a mouth falls open
unknowing pillow
the limits of powder,

the mirror's silver
like a grainy nightmare,
heavy-lipped

blue-fingered, no speaking
from the world's teeth.
Remember the particular words

issuing in the green singing
at the river's mouth. The silted
horizon grows empty,

pock-marked, within reach.
A taste for rice remains
in the mouth's bowl,

goodbye body—
a simple fall.

5.

Above the Golden Gate, a lunar mouth;
where we see a face with bruised blue
eyes in the full moon, in China they see
the profile of a white rabbit pounding rice.
The sliver rim sinks towards the horizon
which has gone from pink to midnight

and now, bedding down for the night
without knowing what will appear—a mouth
falling open like an old woman's, the horizon
of age arriving, the limit of endlessness, the blue
of a grandmother's hair coloring the pillow, rice
powder tinting faded cheeks, her face I see

in the mirror's flat silver, only now I see
it's my face, heavy with the onset of night,
counting out hours like grains of rice.
I can't complain, life has been kind, no mouth
like the nightmare one to swallow me, blue-
lipped, opening on another mouth whose horizon

lies beyond a hideous tongue and teeth, a horizon
beyond which nothing exists, swallowed in a sea—
I'm one small grain on the world's tongue. Blue
flannel blanket I'll pull up at midnight,
gnarled hands beneath my chin, now mouthing
what words I remember, particulate as rice,

one grain on the tongue, in the throat. Rice
issued from the paddies, green filled the horizon,
stooping farmers sang in the silted mouth
of a river delta, water as far as I could see
and the belly empties and growls in the night
and the uncalloused hands ache with their blue-

veined backs. Everyone comes to this heavy blue
air with no appetite left but a taste for rice.
Boys are told to empty the rice bowl each night
lest they marry a pock-marked bride. The horizon
kisses the steely ocean and one by one I see
rice grains fall into the unspeakable mouth,

mouthing a goodbye towards the blue ether.
See—then the body, simple as rice
crosses the known horizon, falls away into night.

Valle d'Aosta

1.

Hollow cowbells rise up from the valley
long before cows appear in the mountains,
a random music like unstill water,
floating up from cold trenches to islands
of warmth on the high slopes beyond cities'
sounds, the low brass notes speak an animal sorrow

and descending we feel the sorrow
as our own. After a day of altitude, the valley
is pulling us homeward toward the trek's end, a city's
black and gold-spangled night, but in the mountains
you and I are just bodies walking through islands
of hours. Lunch: bread and salmon, plums and water,

restored for the afternoon, low on precious water
we remember the day we hadn't filled up, our sorrow
about how many euros per bottle at one of those islands
of civilization, a lift station, liftless. The valley
is reachable by foot, no rides in September's mountains,
the funivia is closed for repairs and tomorrow the city's

lights won't disappear as we leave the five little cities
and ascend, carried up over ridges and ibex, water-
heavy fog surrounds us, we're lost in the mountains,
cloud-bound. A stone marker, some climber's sorrow,
there must be a trail here somewhere to the valley's
moss, I examine rocks for the red/white marks, islands

of logic, a map in the sea of granite islands
above the fog-floor, chirring marmots inhabit cities
of boulders. We've been absorbed into time's valleys,
slipstreams within crags, silvered like water
pooling and sluicing over, spilling into old sorrows,
into crevices between memory and the absent mountains

of a flatland childhood. Before I ever saw mountains
they loomed, heaps of gravel and snow, islands
floating above towns we knew, the everyday pains, sorrows
of what people unknowingly do to each other, cities
of the starved, accumulations of neglect, bacteria in black water,
the battered shape of a child looking for some human valley,

a home from which to wander into valleys, mountains
and glaciers, melted turquoise water, muddy islands
of human cities, moving out of and into blunt sorrow.

(The end-words are taken from W. H. Auden's "Paysage Moralisé")

2.

Cows ascend like unstill music,
up from cold-trenched cities
to the slopes, a low brass sorrow.

After altitude and descending
we're pulled homeward by cold-spangled night,
just walking bodies of salmon and plums,

restored, a precious afternoon. How many euros
per island? Civilization, liftless. The funivia
is closed for September, reachable repairs.

The five cities won't disappear like trails
into wateriness in the fog-bound mountains.
The mossy marker, a climber lost somewhere

in the sea of granite, marmots absorbed
into time. Chirring water spills and sluices over
into sleep's crevices, memory and absence

of a mountain, childhood. Heaps of gravel and snow
float unknowingly above the everyday shapes
of starvation, battles, neglected valleys,

a wandering home, turquoise cities
where humans move like glaciers.

3.

Trenches of animal sound.
Unstill brass music rises up
from the warm cows

pulled into altitude's
black body of night,
salmon's plum bodies,

how many afternoons lifted?
Precious civilization unreachable,
no repairs for September.

The water-heavy cities
disappear like mountains,
cloud-bound, a climber's lost moss

absorbed in a sea of chirring,
marmots spilling into crevices
of memory and absence,

childhood's heaps of unknowing,
looking for snowy valleys
floating above everyday neglect,

blunt wandering starvation,
muddy human sorrow.

4.

Brass cities raise up
random music

into altitude's salmon mountains
and plum-spangled night,

civilization—unreachable,
how many funivias restored?

A climber disappears like ibex
in water-heavy moss

absence absorbed in a sea
of chirring memory

of unknowing valleys
and neglected looking,

turquoise glaciers wandering.

5.

Bell-spangled music
in random plum mountains

a climber—unreachable,
how many civilizations lost?

Memory absorbs ibex
and the sea's absence,

 a valley of blunt neglect.

6.

Climbing plum mountains,
lost valley—unreachable,
how many glaciers?

Real Time

1.

Purple doves reeling,
saturated night, locked house,
sudden white feathers.

2.

A sudden cooing
beside the bed—

time's crooked quaking
theatrical rain
fishes and downspouts

dream: shadowy planets
night's sheltered window.

3.

A black thought:
the sudden bottom

always impending,
bed slipping,

the big bang,
time's crooked reel

creatures' peculiar span,
unspeakable theater

raining white absence,
feathers continuing

dream a shadow's hair—
the web—a fool's window

beyond counting—
night and nothing.

4.

Clearly falling, your hand,
suddenly, a turtle in rain
making its way.

Swept up, an impending
day slipping into
quaking, accruing

time's rough start,
a cycle—rain, sun,
an endless pulse reeling,

peculiar creatures, sun, sun,
obituaries of time, finite as rain,
unspeakably vivid.

Boggy rain, the white cranes
mating, eggs and water,
real lavender continuing,

an unimagined house,
black braids spun into a web.
Remember the galoshes,

a pair sleeping,
shelter, our counting.

5.

Black-bottomed clouds break open, clear rain
falls through. In your hand, is it real?
As real as the turtle doves, the gray pair
cooing, mating dance on sycamore limb, day
making its sudden way into night.
We thought there would be more.

Being swept up into something more,
hazards accumulate as time does, as rain
accrues its own fog, saturating night,
cooling our skin, weighting worries with real
earthquakes, pandemics, gamma rays, days
of impending illness, slippers waiting for a pair

of feet, the crooked little toe, the pair
of calluses. Tenderness? Wanting more.
Maybe the big bang, time's rough start, day
out of nothing. Probably a cycle, rain
then sun, an exploded pulse, the endless reel;
why should we have it any different than night

falling down on the other creatures? Purple night,
peculiar roilings, sun up, sun down, another pair.
Planets circle the globe. We wanted theater, real
ends, as in the *Times* obituaries, more
vivid lives (war pilot, Channel swimmer, dancer, spy). Rain
taps on the terra cotta roof, filling downspouts daily,

flattening the lavender into the boggy grass. Day
slicks down the white crane's feathers, all night
perched in his scraggly tree, waiting for another rain
of fishes and water, nests and eggs, the mated pair
lost, one gone and the other continuing, more
absence, half of the nest not slept in. A reel

of leaves and water, time's tanglings, more real
than imagined—the dream of a locked house, day
remote, black windows, the shadow of her head, more
wild hair, braided and let go, a web spun out into night.
The window opens, someone speaks, remember, a pair
of galoshes—we went there, soaking, into the next rain

and on beyond into rain after rain towards real
loss, a pair of fools sheltered for a day,
night after night, counted hours, nothing more.

The Forest

1.

Children born in a time of calm
walk differently, not hugging the walls
as they walk down school corridors, not
startling to any percussive sound.
You sleep in a soft flannel bed, imagining forests
and dragons, three wishes, talking

animals, the wolf who swallows the talking
grandmother who is disinterred by a calm
axeman. Refound in the dense bamboo forest,
she tells the children stories of stone walls
in which doorways open without a sound
into the ground and you enter, not

without fear, leaving a trail of breadcrumbs, not
without sorrow as you part with the talking
carp whose golden scales mirror the sound
of sunlight. And below ground, pools of calm
moonlight reflect off the water seeping from walls
made of chalk. You realize, beneath this forest

they buried the bodies of the lost ones, a forest
of rifles once stood here, an army serving not
the benevolent emperor but the one who built walls
and pushed scholars and poets into pits still talking
and covered them over after stealing calmly
their children, their gold and teeth. No sound

escaped from the vanished ones. No live sound
of voices among the foxes and owls of the forest.
Memory is a language of echoes, the face of calm
is nothing but hollowness, an empty ringing, not
in the ears but the chest. Someone keeps talking
about portraits of the dead hung on the walls,

who look down at the sleeping child, walls
painted with blue clouds, murmuring sounds,
wind chimes, behind each voice, a dead voice talking
about eating bread crumbs, starving in the forest.
The parents went out and never returned, in a knot
of fear, while the child was hidden inside a calm

house, held in calm arms which formed ivied walls
encircling not this child but the lost one, storied sound,
crying in the forest, ghosts hug the walls, talking.

2.

Dream three wishes in imaginary
calm, not startling dragons
in corridors sound,

the grandmother swallows the axeman
who tells stories in which
stone turns into bamboo,

you part with the breadcrumbs,
scales mirror the ground,
moonlight on walls made of water,

the body of the lost emperor
is buried in a pit, steely rifles talking,
children covered in gold

among foxes and owls. Memory
is a language of ringing,
empty echoes in the chest,

the murmur of chimed voices,
parents painting,
sleeping children return

to the ivied house,
hugged in ghostly arms.

3.

In the school for dragons,
startling percussion,

a carp tells stories
in the doorway. Stony sounds

seep from below ground,
the moon writes in chalk

for benevolent scholars.
In a forest of teeth

escaped from vanishing,
the old portraits ring

with dead parents,
murmurs of hidden children

encircled by dark, starved
in a forest of talking.

4.

In a time of difference
someone opens a door

to the wolf.
Scaled mirror, sorrow

a forest of buried bodies
the owls' language echoes

ghosts speaking
in old arms in the dark.

5.
Sunlight's army, starved
bodies, sorrow's open door—
a forest, a ghost.

Muddy Hollow

1.

Untranslated light
maps the other hemisphere,
the mind's braided whirl.

2.

Throaty ocean
translates cargo
downhill—

luxuries lost,
the other hemisphere's
wetland map.

3.

Camouflaged arrival
of the clouds' ocean

a rumpled language
dropping its cargo of *r's*

converting need into cash
good will into rayon

ungoverned cowslips dip
in the marshland's whirl

a state of enduring
unshaped glints, dissolved beings

the impossible world
beyond pattern.

4.

Sun-splashed notes of bird-song,
throat-piercing, shadow-dappling
song is a camouflaged ocean,

untranslatable, brush-worked hills.
Language contains the swept texture
of dropped sounds beyond the ears'

store, converting goodwill into a whirl
of exchanges. Yellow dresses
flow hungrily downhill.

Beyond reach, the map,
to our regret, sound swallows
light, painted grasses,

water, what the mind does with it,
unshaped shapes in the ungoverned
hemisphere, the foreign eye

noting the arrival of light,
of a billion small fates,
while geography is flying

through a patterned mind,
the pelted darkness.

5.

Sun-splashed green reeds, silver pond, a whirl
of red-wings and their throaty notes,
piercing calls, the clouds' dappled shadows,
reflected camouflage, wind-struck water, arriving
one by one, the light, the birds, the song, governed
by half-seen forces, a mottled ocean beyond

the hills like rumpled felt, and beyond
that far sweep, mistranslated nations, a whirl
of languages, brush work, incense, governed
by tone, Cantonese, nine, Mandarin, four notes
to sound the texture of *sh's, z's, r*-slurred arrivals
on an alien ear. Container ships drop cargo, shadowed

by ICE, uncounted people hidden in shadows,
hungry commerce, convertibles in numbers beyond
need, tennis shoes, yellow rayon dresses, new arrivals
in the Goodwill store, sent back across the ocean, a whirl
of exchange and loss, fierce need. It's been noted
how commodities flow uphill, cash-governed,

rolling towards whoever has. We're lost. The map governed
us but still, that rising hill shouldn't be shadowing
the marshland. White egret sounds one harsh note,
unfolds, flies off, swallows dip and swirl just beyond
reach, fine gnats precede them, cowslips' lacy whirl,
paintbrush, grasses. Were we hoping for arrival—

a state of being, constant and enduring? What arrives—
water and what the wind does with it, ungoverned
intersecting circles of light and dark, a whirl
of unshaped shapes, glints dissolve into shadows,
the other hemisphere, foreign sounds, beyond
the easy eye, the listening ear, lost echo, a note

of loss, ours and the far world's. We note
and go on seeing. It's all one place arriving
at the possible, impossible-but-lived lives beyond
one being's grasp, ten billion fates ungoverned,
tin-roofed houses, small luxury of sautéed chicken, shadows
of birds flying over wetlands, geography's print and whirl

the whirl of mind, braid-patterned lines, a note
of mauve shadow on the pelted hills, arrival
of a governed darkness—this order, this beyond.

Plunge

1.
Dive in, greet the turquoise blue
embrace, become a firm shape floating
in the deep end, let little waves
break over your skin as you reach
for the tiled wall, follow the black line
down the lane towards the next turn

arrive at another lap, turbulent flip-turn,
swimming back the way you came. Blue,
light ripples crossing your own line
of waves, reflect, refract, rock a leaf floating
on the surface of the invisible world, reach
for something solid as a wall, bounce waves

off the barrier to intersect with other waves.
Each moment's wake creates the next turn
and you're again inside a body. You reach
outside. What's a membrane anyway? The blue
rim that never appeared in a world that floats
from one trouble to the next, drawing lines

in "ethnic cleansing," Poland's shifting border lines,
police on horses push at strikers, freed prisoners wave,
sand dunes without life forms, smoke floating
in from the last war. Why will one people turn
against another, not once in every blue
moon, but always somewhere? We reach

forward in our efforts to be good, to reach
a place where bad is on the other side of the line
and we are here, buoyant, paddling around in blue
pools, not to be disturbed, eyes closed, waving
goodbye to a part of ourselves, trying to turn
inside out, into something blameless, to float

free and name the other bad, letting us float
down the river of hopefulness. But we reach
a place where the worst is possible, even to turn
into what we say we despise. All lines
delineate shadow, each rising wave
of history erases the last, gone under, blue

water washes blue light, you blithely float
down the waves' crest and froth, reaching
for the slippery bottom, the shoreline, breath's turn.

2.

Blue. Embrace turns into shape,
wavelets follow your skin,
tiled firmness, the black line

arrives at turbulence. Reflect on
the floating from which you came. Light
refracts on a leaf, your visible surface

intersects with a moment's wake.
Inside a body, who is waving
in a world of trouble creating lines

between dunes, police, lines of death
without cleansing, left smoking
after the war against Poland?

We've disturbed the old lakes,
waving goodbye to our bad selves,
turning blame inside out.

Reaching down the despised river
all lines delineate shadow,
each rising wave of memory erases us,

water washes down the bottom,
froth on the shoreline's light.

3.

Your skin is a broken wall
greeting the black waves

another flip-turn refracts surface light
the way you came, invisible

intersections with trouble
a moment's appearance wakes the world.

Between wars without history
membranes float without life

and we're paddling, not disturbing
our blameless selves, turned upside down

delineating the river of what's possible.
All lines erase shadow

washing the shoreline, where
water marries bottom.

4.

Dive into the turquoise skin
of surface light, reflect on
a moment's body, intersecting troubles

a smoky truce disturbs
our blithe breath

rising waves delineate hope,
washing the shadow's shore.

5.

Watery shadow—
our blue breath reflected on
war's cresting moment.

Burial

1.

Underground, the box—
a visible marriage, earth's
continents, one body.

2.

Gladioli strike the coffin,
sun swirling

daughter marries her phone
a window on loyalty

a dying peach inviting
future death, fathering emptiness

generation is muscular
children hollow

breath's calligraphy
on the body's scroll.

3.

Gazing at the hill fires
sun lowering, underground

at 90, time is a slow school
memory peripheral. The young lack

the calligrapher's faint skill. A hole
in loyalty opens, the widow's amnesia

follows. Earnest hands, sugary invitations
we all knew the time,

an empty sandwich. Breath
is the lungs' story

the hole closes, claims
new and constant bodies

ink slides into April
washing sight.

4.

Six children shovel earth,
the hole's funereal hollow,
underground's ritual smoke,

92 slow years, a fading art.
Young cousins lack memory
of Uncle's sprightly driving.

The widow's daughters
are loyal, with amnesia for healing,
for hollowing, they forget that

the future is dying hair and spotted
arms. Canton marries Sugarland,
war-time: our time.

Ten generations remembered,
the dynasty's imprint on muscles,
tending towards vacancy,

a step-father's death is constantly
reclaimed, the list of calligraphers
empties, watches unwind,

stillness hollows the mind,
death's black scroll.

5.

Hollow, the mechanism of gladioli, too sunny
for lowering smoke, for fires underground.
Time and ritual tie children to coffins

of peripheral elders. The canyons' slow
calligraphy hollows a fading LA
as we drive at 80 to the artful cousin's

whose granddaughters are loyal to their phones.
Married to amnesia, the widow scrolls through
photos, the faint war-time faces she's out-lasted,

earnest and sugary, the peachy aunts,
the hollow future of New York, the long
arms of the Cantonese, inviting and timely.

Sandwiched between generations, we eat
the imprint of vacant space, follow old stories,
which preceded us across continents, hold

our rewritten youth in place, march onto the list
we constantly watch, calibrating the nearness
of our bodies to the still-time, the breath-hole,

the inky spill of the throat's aspirations,
the mind's final hold.

6.

At his uncle TY's funeral, we gaze into the hole,
well over six feet, the lowering mechanism still
in place. Children throw gladioli on the box in sight
underground. Then the ritual shovel of earth, hollow
sound as it strikes coffin wood. Too sunny, time
swirls in with thin smoke from the hill fires, scrolls

into the canyons of LA's periphery. Inside, scrolls
of calligraphy done by the elders, a whole
generation's skill fading out in the young who lack time
for the slow arts. We drive the other uncle, still
sprightly at 92, he re-meets grade school cousins, hollow
memory, he's not seen them for 80 years. Sight

has remained loyal, out-lasting his hearing. Sightly
granddaughters in spike heels take photos, scroll
through their iPhones to show us TY's faint, hollow
face. The widow has been waiting for this hole
in her life to open, after years of his amnesia, still
she wanted his life at hand. Married during war-time,

they invited all the Cantonese they knew at the time
in New York, Hong Yuen who would, in a future out of sight,
marry uncle's younger sister Ton To (Ernest Peach). Still,
looking at the Sugarland Auntie's dyed black hair, we scroll
along her arms to the brown-spotted hands, hold
in mind, these are our hands soon, hollowing

muscles, tendons growing visible. Breath is hollow
in the lungs of the living eating little sandwiches, time
to remember, stories across continents, generations hold
the imprint of those who preceded, hold in sight
these who will follow TY, oldest of ten children. Scroll
into the present, we shift up into the vacant space, stillness

ahead of us, growing into the skin of the elders, still
not quite sure. In April, burying my step-father, a hollow
place still empty in mind where the new death arrives, a scroll
constantly rewritten, each name added to the list in time's
faded calligraphy notes us moving more fully into sight,
our bodies closer to that hole, our breath claiming hold

of what still aspires. The black inky wash of time
spills into the hollow of a throat, spreads to cover sight,
scrolls into the mind's folds that hold the dead now, whole.

Postcard

1.

Dears: We landed in a frozen world,
Ohio ice prisming dazed branches,
we walked beside a green-black river,
a snow-hidden hill, smelling the wet
rich air, earth preparing mulch, its
involution, a reburst of rising. Old,

we have flown far from our bold
selves, shed skins in a world
flagging, ochering its colors, its
water table sinking. Our way branched
more than we imagined, feet wet
with fluid of our birthing, the river

crossed, serpentine and icy, the river
became a stream, became a stalky field. Old
silver planes have rusted in the wet
air, having served time in the world's
battles between faith's branches,
now shells, grounded and flightless. It's

a place we hoped not to recognize. It's
constant, our grief for the hours' river,
for slippage, for memory that branches
down tangential pathways into old
familiar corners and bizarre worlds.
The story: born pink and wet,

we wobbled, reached, grew erect, wet
membranes separated us from danger and its
intrusions; still the edges of others' worlds
pierced our flesh. Once natural like the river
which leaves its spring, departs from old
mountains and descends in myriad branches

into cataracts, canyons, gullies, branches
like veins returning to the heart, to wet
reed beds, plains of egrets, the ocean's old
mollusks, we're swept up by time, its
tidal troughs, tributaries to the river
of leaving and arrival in this world

of bodies, a world of history, the branches
of a molten river inside our wet selves, licking
us with its old tongue into being.

2.

Ice prisms on the rising river,
smelling the snowy air,
earth's frozen mulch,

we traveled far from our sinking
selves. Black branches,
a river of our ocher,

battles of flags and crosses,
the silver planes balked,
we lost faith—

an old story. Memory,
bizarre pathway,
recognizes slipping hours

intrusions separated us
from the piercing river,
mountainous nature departed.

Returning veins, cataracts,
sweep the heart's gullies,
time's troughs and tributaries

arrive in the branching world,
a wet being, history's body.

3.

A smell on the air's snowy river
frozen prism of earth

sinking far from our shed selves
the river of flags

became a rusted plane
our faith flightless

memory's old story
grief's old tangents

wobbling mountains
separated us from the departed

cataracts and tributaries
swept history's canyons

a tongue licks the heart
its molten veins.

4.

Ohio's involution
into green-black mulch

a lost water table
stalked by streaming battles

recognizing the world's slip
flesh departs in Spring

history's branching river.

5.

Shedding stalky green
skin, lost rivers branching from birth—
memory's old tongue.

Hike

1.

Glacial pools in scree,
lapping grave immersion, sheen,
time's bright element.

2.

September's vacation undone,
our cells' electricity fading

water view, fate is unphotographed,
light's shimmer circumscribed

looking is liquid, accessible
up to our waists in weather

a confluence doesn't follow.

3.

Snow-dust undone by sun-glare,
ambulation undone by basins

fishermen biopsy the big lake's
circumference, yawn, wait.

Marmots move into condos
circumventing filmed meadows,

nature's drama of light-slap-rock,
water-pool-on-granite, elemental planes

of glacial stances, unseen landslides,
sheer inclines give way to scree

aspen retrace the daylight
no longer here, orogeny

means gravel finds altitude
immersed in air.

4.

Winter undoes our Sierra September
vacation, snow-glare, release from
nestling, from sealing in

we're light and regular, not yawning,
not high. Fish in saddlebags
let loose their electricity, lake-shimmer

the glee of blankness, fateful mica,
we are creatures who photograph
every lake, windy and tree-line. Up

in the elemental planes of rock,
pools of nothing continuous,
waves' light oozes into the photo.

On an elusive incline, the mind
gives way, accessible to delight,
switching back from ground to liquid

navigating the day's yellow, going on
into weather, Triassic pines, retracing
lines of beaver-felled trees

circumstantial glaciers
which did not go on being.

5.

Eastern Sierra, Twenty Lake Basin trail, alpine lake
after snow-dusted lake, gullies, sun-glare, the last
day of September, winter comes early to the high
country. We set out to circumambulate
on the last day of vacation, release about
to be undone, resealing us into our quotidian path

lately weighty and frayed, a tortuous path,
waiting for biopsy results. First is Saddlebag Lake,
flat azure, early fishermen, creels yawning for fish about
to be caught. Lightened by our news: benign, we'll last
a bit longer, fear fading, electricity let loose. Circumflex
shore line, sun-shimmer beyond the big lake, higher

meadows at tree-line, marmot cry, creatures used to high
living, rock condos, crystalline air, water view. The windy path
curves past unnamed ponds, the glee of circumventing
fate carries us, scree-fields, mica-glint, Blank Lake.
Nothing goes unphotographed, boulders of basalt, clast,
now he's found the Leica's movie-function, one minute about

water, lap-slap of liquid on rock, rippling is about
radiance, sine waves, intersecting planes, the high
drama of nothing happening but molecules' humming, lasting,
elemental. I'm now Mrs. Ozu, waiting by the path
for his films' completion, slow as Ozu, low as Ozu. Lakes
of light pooling in granite, glacial carvings circumfused

with snow-melt, formed over millennia. Our circumstance:
sun and how the body uses it, the mind's delight about
taking in, still breathing. In yesterday's snow, Helen Lake
was not quite accessible. The final switchback in scree, high
up on a sheer wet incline, we stopped to find the elusive path
and resting there, a little landslide. Ground gave way and at last

our will did, turning back to retrace our steps in the last
translucence, in pine and yellow aspen, circumnavigating
beaver dams, felled trees up to their waists in water, the path
sank below tree-line, we saw no one in such weather. About
to be, having been, going on being, the Paiute no longer here, high
in a home country sculpted by the Nevadan orogeny, Triassic lakes,

the glaciers which did not last, we who are about
to leave, immersed in the bright circumfluent high altitude
air, follow the gravelly path back to the first lake.

Time Change

1.
Evening arrives with its sorry orange
glow, time and its sadness, the heavy
workings, another turn of the wheel
and we're off into the pastels of night-fall,
always saying goodbye to the light,
always goodbye, *joy-geen,* see you again

in the morning, and we'll close our eyes again
and envision the waterfall and the oranges
filled with sweetness and their own light.
We eat until fullness, become heavy
as the moon we sleep underneath, fall
into ourselves in darkness. And the wheel

revolves. I rise, dress, sit behind the wheel,
clean, in stockings and real shoes again,
off into the changing weather at a new hour, fall
having arrived before I was ready, orange
maples, full of the extra hour of sleep, heavy-
lidded, full of my own dream while light

breaks on the dreams of others. Lamp-light,
closed space, one red window, one hour wheels
into the next, layers of mind interwoven, heavy
with spectral textures. A moment again
evolves into the next, a scent of orange
remains from lunch, fills the room, dusk falls

early, still listening for what comes, footfalls
of the years, what sense we've made, what light
has fallen on the canyon of unknowns. An orange
lucency fills the room, one small space wheels
through the galaxy, a cube inside a spiral, again
reeling into some place new, outside the heavy

history of our journey, outside the heavy
origins of human tangents. Leaving, scent of fall
leaves, red on the pavement, rain coming again,
home to him and the cats, warm greetings, light
incense, bow to the bodhisattva, word-wheels,
chants for the liquid of compassion in her orange

flowered jar. Oranges for dessert, sleep-heavy,
the day wheels into October's dark, we fall
into bed, lights out, plunge into depths again.

Fall again—light's heavy orange wheel.

2.

Orange glow of sadness
a turn of pastels,
joy's heavy wheel.

Eyeing the fullness
inside sleep's waterfall, we fall
into sweet darkness and the light

revolves. We rise into weather,
new orange maples,
a heavy-lidded hour

night wheels, interwoven
lamp light, textured space,
red window, a spectral scent,

the downfall of leaves. One
small spiral reeling
into canyons of the human,

the rain's red greeting
on the pavement
the bodhisattva's liquid incense,

October's dark flowers
wheel into day.

3.

"See you again"
the workings of goodbye

underneath a waterfall
we eat in darkness

rise into an extra hour
of weather, orange maples

interwoven, text of lamp light
one red window remaining

lucent, listen
for footfalls of the galaxy

tangled scent of red leaves
the bodhisattva rain

day's fall into
sleep-heavy October.

4.

Goodbye: wheeling
into watery darkness

an extra hour of maples
a woven red glow

the galaxy's small wheels
tangled leaves

October's flowered jar.

5.

Goodbye to darkness—
the galaxy's wheel plunges
maples into red.

ALICE JONES'S books are *The Knot* from Alice James Books, *Extreme Directions (The fifty four moves of Tai Chi Sword)* published by Omnidawn, and *Gorgeous Mourning*. Her chapbooks are *Isthmus* and *Anatomy*. Her poems have appeared in *Ploughshares, Poetry, Boston Review, Volt, Denver Quarterly, Kenyon Review, Verse,* and in anthologies including *Best American Poetry of 1994; Blood and Bone: Poems by Doctors; Verse* and *Universe: Poems about Science* and *Strange Attraction: A ZYZZYVA Anthology.*

Her awards include fellowships from the Bread Loaf Writers Conference and the National Endowment for the Arts, the First Annual Narrative Magazine Poetry Prize, and the Robert H. Winner and Lyric Poetry Awards from the Poetry Society of America. She practices psychoanalysis in Berkeley and is a supervising and personal analyst at the San Francisco Center for Psychoanalysis and the Psychoanalytic Institute of Northern California.

OTHER POETRY TITLES
FROM APOGEE PRESS

Maxine Chernoff
Among the Names
The Turning

Valerie Coulton
The Cellar Dreamer
open book
passing world pictures

Tsering Wangmo Dhompa
In the Absent Everyday
My rice tastes like the lake
Rules of the House

Kathleen Fraser
Discrete Categories Forced into
Coupling

Paul Hoover
Edge and Fold

Alice Jones
Gorgeous Mourning

Stefanie Marlis
cloudlife
fine

Edward Kleinschmidt Mayes
Speed of Life

Pattie McCarthy
bk of (h)rs
Table Alphabetical of Hard Words
Verso

Denise Newman
Human Forest
Wild Goods

Elizabeth Robinson
Also Known As
Apostrophe
Apprehend

Edward Smallfield
equinox
The Pleasures of C

Cole Swensen
Oh

Truong Tran
dust and conscience
four letter words
placing the accents
within the margin

TO ORDER OR FOR MORE
INFORMATION GO TO
WWW.APOGEEPRESS.COM